Puerto Rico

JoAnn Milivojevic

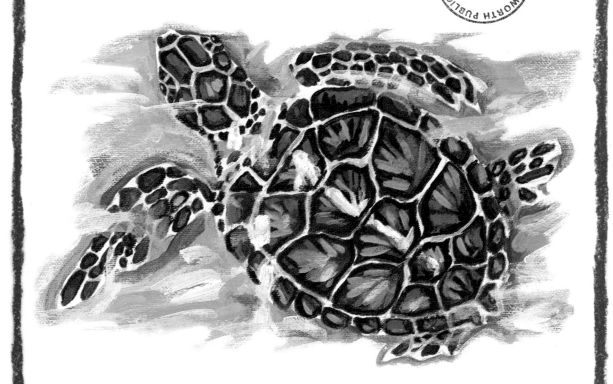

✒ Carolrhoda Books, Inc. / Minneapolis

500470639

Photo Acknowledgments

Photos, maps, and artworks are used courtesy of: John Erste, pp. 1, 2–3, 6–7, 13, 26–27, 39; Laura Westlund, pp. 4–5, 37; © Mark Bacon, pp. 6, 7 (both), 8–9, 10, 13, 19 (top), 21 (left), 29 (right), 30 (both), 31, 36, 40 (both), 41, 43 (left); © Eugene Schulz, p. 9 (top); © Thomas R. Fletcher, pp. 9 (bottom), 19 (bottom); © Jaime Santiago/DDB Stock Photo, p. 11 (top); © Suzanne Murphy-Larronde/DDB Stock Photo, pp. 11 (bottom), 16 (both), 25; Knights of Columbus Headquarters Museum, p. 12; Puerto Rico General Archives, p. 14; © Richard B. Levine, p. 17; © Robert Fried, pp. 18, 27, 26, 34, 34–35, 37, 38; © Tony Arruza, pp. 20, 22, 24; © D. Donne Bryant/DDB Stock Photo, p. 21 (right); © TRIP/R. C. Fournier, p. 23; © Bob Krist/The Puerto Rico Tourism Co., pp. 28, 29 (left), 39; © Joan Iaconetti, pp. 32, 42, 43 (right); © W. Lynn Seldon Jr./DDB Stock Photo, p. 33; Pittsburgh Pirates, p. 35; Cover photo of Puerto Rican kids by © Suzanne Murphy-Larronde/DDB Stock Photo.

Carolrhoda Books, Inc.
A Division of Lerner Publishing Group
241 First Avenue North
Minneapolis, Minnesota 55401 U.S.A.

Website address: www.lernerbooks.com

Words in **bold type** are explained in a glossary that begins on page 44.

Library of Congress Cataloging-in-Publication Data

Milivojevic, JoAnn.
    Puerto Rico / by JoAnn Milivojevic.
        p. cm. — (A ticket to)
    Includes index.
    Summary: Provides an overview of the geography, people, language, customs, religion, lifestyle, and culture of Puerto Rico.
    ISBN 1-57505-144-3 (lib. bdg. : alk. paper)
    1. Puerto Rico—Juvenile literature. [1. Puerto Rico.]
I. Title. II. Series.
F1958.3.M56 2000
972.95—dc21   98-39109

Manufactured in the United States of America
1 2 3 4 5 6 – JR – 05 04 03 02 01 00

Contents

Welcome!

Four **islands** make up the **U.S. commonwealth** of Puerto Rico. The biggest island is called Puerto Rico. (No surprise there!) The Atlantic Ocean soaks its northern and eastern coasts. The warmer Caribbean Sea bathes its southern and western shores. Two smaller islands, Vieques and Culebra, rest off Puerto Rico's eastern coast. Mona Island lies off to the west.

Map Whiz Quiz

Look at the map on page 5. Trace the inset map (in the box) onto a piece of paper. Find Sierra de Luquillo. Mark that side of your paper with an *E* for east. Find Ponce and put an *S* for south. Put an *N* for north near Arecibo. Shade in the water around Puerto Rico to make it an island.

PUERTO RICO

San Juan
Loíza
Arecibo
Carolina
El Yunque
SIERRA DE LUQUILLO
N
CORDILLERA CENTRAL
Ponce
Guayama

Miles
0   10   20
0   10   20   30
Kilometers

mountains
foothills
karst
lowlands
semidesert
rain forest
★ capital city

ATLANTIC
OCEAN

Culebra
Puerto Rico
Mona
Vieques

COMMONWEALTH OF
PUERTO RICO

C A R I B B E A N   S E A

Mangroves, trees that grow in muddy saltwater areas, thrive along parts of Puerto Rico's coastline.

Ups and Downs

Beaches and **coves** edge Puerto Rico's coasts. In the northern coastal lowlands, farmers raise sugarcane and pineapples. The sun bakes southeastern Puerto Rico. Not much grows there! Mountains push up in the

Parts of Puerto Rico are covered with a landscape called karst. Over millions of years, underground streams hollowed out caves in the limestone (a soft rock). In some caves, the ceilings collapsed, making big **craters** in the earth's surface. In one of those craters, scientists built Arecibo Observatory. It has the largest radio-radar telescope on earth. It is 1,000 feet across!

Bumpy karst landscape in northern Puerto Rico

middle of the island. The Cordillera Central **mountain range** runs from east to west. The Sierra de Luquillo mountains lie in the northeast.

Wet Weather

Puerto Rico has a **tropical** climate. Temperatures stay about 82 degrees all year round. Ocean breezes help keep people cool. Sometimes huge storms called **hurricanes** strike the island. But during most of the year, Puerto Rico has mild weather.

In El Yunque, Puerto Rico's **rain forest** in the northeast, plants and flowers grow thick and leafy. Animals, birds, and lots of insects live there.

More than 100 billion gallons of rain fall every year in El Yunque (above).

El Coquí

Puerto Rico's most famous rain forest creature is *el coquí*. This yellowish tree frog is about the size of your pinky finger. Its name comes from the sound it makes as night falls on the forest— "koh-KEE! koh-KEE!"

Hurricanes usually hit Puerto Rico in September. These storms can cause lots of destruction.

9

A young Taino learns to make a tool by hand.

First People

Puerto Rico's first people were the Taino Indians. They called their homeland Borinquén, which means "Island of the Brave Lord." The Tainos grew crops. They fished and hunted wild animals. As many as 40 people shared a large, airy home. Taino artists carved wooden bowls and boxes. From cotton, weavers made belts, clothing, and hammocks.

The Tainos slept in homes built on tall poles. Breezes kept people cool on hot nights.

Meet Me at the Bayete!

The Tainos built villages around large public squares called *bayetes.* There they held festivals, enjoyed dances, and played a ball game similar to soccer. Historians believe the game got its start in Mexico.

Taino traders paddled canoes to nearby islands to swap the handmade goods.

The Tainos warmly greeted the first Spaniards to arrive on their island.

Spanish Settlers

Christopher Columbus claimed Borinquén for Spain in 1493. About 15 years later, settlers came from Spain in search of gold. The Spaniards forced the Tainos to mine for the valuable metal. Many Tainos died from diseases the Spaniards carried. Others left for nearby islands. When the gold ran low, the Spaniards turned to farming coffee, sugarcane, and tobacco. Spanish farmers

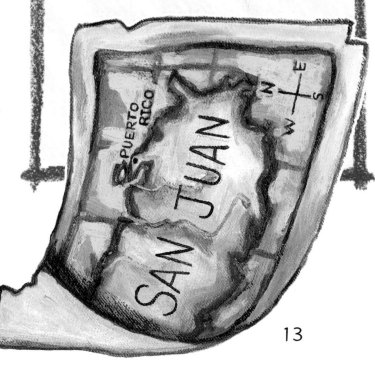

The Spaniards admired the Tainos' handmade pottery.

Name Switcheroo!

Columbus renamed Borinquén "San Juan Bautista" in honor of a Roman Catholic saint. The first Spanish town on the island was named Puerto Rico ("rich port" in Spanish). Some historians think that an early mapmaker switched the names on the map. The island came to be called Puerto Rico, and the town San Juan.

made the Tainos work on plantations (large farms) and brought slaves from Africa to work in the fields.

13

Changing Hands

During Spanish rule, cities and towns sprang up. Farming and trading grew. People built churches, fancy homes, and shops. The early Spanish settlers had many things in common with people in Spain. But over time, they came to see themselves as Puerto Ricans and wanted independence. Spain slowly gave the islanders freedom.

Puerto Rico's first president, Luis Muñoz Rivera

What is a Commonwealth?

As citizens of a U.S. commonwealth, Puerto Ricans can travel freely between Puerto Rico and the United States. They use U.S. money and follow U.S. laws. The United States protects Puerto Rico. Puerto Ricans cannot vote for U.S. president, but they do not pay tax money. Many Puerto Ricans like this arrangement. Others want independence. Still others want Puerto Rico to become a U.S. state. Once in a while, islanders vote on who should rule their homeland. In 1998 they voted to stay a commonwealth.

The Puerto Rican flag

In 1898 Luis Muñoz Rivera became Puerto Rico's first president. But independence was short. The United States won a war with Spain and took over Puerto Rico. In 1952 the island became a U.S. commonwealth.

Proud People

Puerto Ricans are proud of their island home. They consider themselves Puerto Ricans first and U.S. citizens second. One Puerto Rican may look very different from another. **Ethnic**

Puerto Ricans of all ethnic backgrounds are proud of who they are.

Nuyoricans

Over the years, many Puerto Ricans have chosen to move to the United States—some in search of jobs, others to go to college. The largest group of Puerto Ricans in the United States lives in New York City. They call themselves Nuyoricans.

Puerto Ricans have **ancestors** from one or more of the island's three **ethnic groups.** Puerto Ricans with high cheekbones and dark eyes have Taino roots. Others with darker skin have African ancestors. Those with blond hair or blue eyes have Spanish backgrounds.

Nearly one million people live in San Juan.

City Slickers

About seven of every ten Puerto Ricans live in a city. City folks typically live in one-family homes or in tall apartment buildings. Life is modern for people in cities. Lots of families have televisions, radios, and computers. Most city people live in bustling San Juan.

Cars and buses whiz through the streets. People hurry to work in high-rise office buildings and browse in shopping centers.

San Juan holds many festivals and parades. Carnival is a Roman Catholic holiday.

Yesterday's City

The oldest part of San Juan looks much the same as it did years ago. The first settlers built the city in the style of cities in Spain. Visitors enjoy touring the narrow cobblestone streets, spotting old houses, and exploring museums that teach about Puerto Rico's history.

On the Farm

Life in Puerto Rico's countryside moves a little slower than city life. Families of six or more people usually share a simple wooden home. Many men farm for a living. They grow food for the family and sell the extra goods at markets. Women often work at home,

A farmer picks green peppers from his garden.

Folks often meet at the colmado to play dominoes.

El Jíbaro

Some of Puerto Rico's early Spaniards left the cities to farm in the countryside. They are called *jíbaros*. Men wore straw hats, white shirts, and loose pants. Women wore colorful skirts and blouses and bright jewelry. Modern-day Puerto Ricans honor the lifestyle of those early Puerto Ricans with parades and festivals.

raising kids and taking care of family business. After a hard day's work, many neighbors enjoy meeting at the *colmado* (village store).

In their free time, families might head to the beach for a barbecue.

Family Matters

In the countryside, families with six or more kids share a home with parents, grandparents, aunts, and uncles. This arrangement is known as an extended family. Everyone helps cook,

All in the Family

Here are the Spanish words for family members. Try them out on your family.

grandfather	*abuelo*	(ah-BWAY-loh)
grandmother	*abuela*	(ah-BWAY-lah)
father	*papi*	(PAH-pee)
mother	*mami*	(MAH-mee)
uncle	*tío*	(TEE-oh)
aunt	*tía*	(TEE-ah)
son	*hijo*	(EE-hoh)
daughter	*hija*	(EE-hah)
brother	*hermano*	(ehr-MAH-noh)
sister	*hermana*	(ehr-MAH-nah)

clean, and tend the garden. Children are taught to respect and obey older family members. Extended families living together are less common in the city.

Festivities for patron saints can last up to 10 days. Folks in Loíza turn out to honor Saint James.

Celebrate!

Most Puerto Ricans are Roman Catholics. Many island celebrations are based on Roman Catholic holidays. For example, most towns and cities in Puerto Rico have a

Roman Catholic patron saint. People believe that the saint looks out for the town and its people. On special days, townspeople honor their patron saint with festivals featuring parades, dancing, and feasts.

Christmastime means presents for Puerto Rican children. They exchange gifts on Three Kings' Day (January 6). Christians believe that three wise kings gave gifts to the baby Jesus on this day.

Kids dress up for Three Kings' Day.

Strictly Speaking

Puerto Ricans speak *español* (Spanish). They added some words from the Taino and English languages. Words like *barbacoa* (barbecue), *hamaca* (hammock), and *canoa* (canoe), come from the Tainos.

Street signs in Puerto Rico appear in Spanish.

The word *huracán* (hurricane) comes from the Taino name Juracan, which means "God of the Fierce Winds."

26

Nuyoricans returning to Puerto Rico brought home some English words, including *liders* (leaders), *elevador* (elevator), and *yarda* (yard).

Speaking Inglés

Many Puerto Ricans speak both Spanish and English. They are **bilingual.** Puerto Ricans who speak English might own businesses or work in hotels and restaurants that attract English-speaking visitors. Many U.S. people visit Puerto Rico each year.

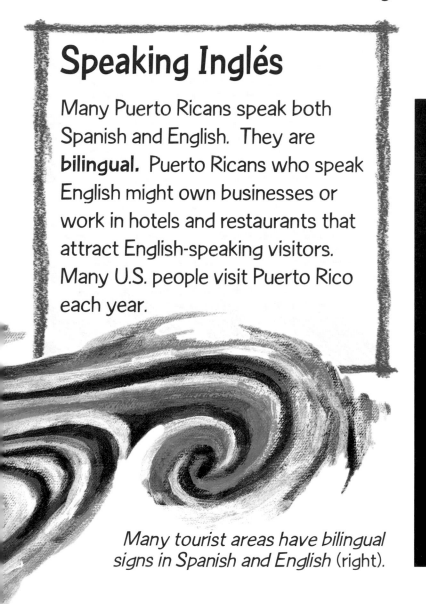

Many tourist areas have bilingual signs in Spanish and English (right).

All Passengers Traveling To The U.S. Mainland Must Present Their Baggage For Inspection By U.S. Agriculture.

Todo Pasajero Que Viaja A Los E.U. Continentales Debe Presentar Su Equipaje Para Inspeccion De Agricultura Federal.

Old Buildings

Some Puerto Rican buildings were made hundreds of years ago. Buildings with fancy balconies, windows, and doorways line cobblestone streets. Puerto Ricans call the southern city of Ponce *"la perla del sur"* (the

pearl of the south). Some buildings in Ponce have rounded corners.

La Fortaleza in San Juan was built in 1522.

A building in Ponce with rounded corners

The curved corners made it easier for horse-drawn carriages to turn through the streets.

El Morro

Many years ago, crafty pirates made the sea around Puerto Rico dangerous. In 1540 builders finished El Morro to protect San Juan. The **fortress** was built on a hill. Its 20-foot-thick walls towered above the sea. Secret tunnels and hiding places lay inside the walls. In 1783 builders finished a wall around the city. The wall still encloses parts of modern-day San Juan.

Time to Eat

Getting hungry? For a snack, try a plate of *tostones*. This Puerto Rican specialty is fried plantains, which are large, starchy bananas. For a hearty meal, try a bowl of asopao—a stew

Stop at a local market for some fresh fruit (left). Or you might prefer a hot plate of tostones (above).

Softball-sized mangoes will fall from the trees as they ripen!

made with vegetables, rice, and meat or fish. Stroll through a large supermarket. Or stop at a small open-air market to buy fresh produce from the people who grew it. A typical Puerto Rican shopping list includes beans, rice, plantains, meat, coffee, eggs, and fruit.

Many kinds of fruit grow in Puerto Rico. Bananas and coconuts are popular. So is the *genip*. It looks like a large grape with a tough outer skin. And everyone loves mangoes! These fruits make great desserts.

Puerto Rican students ride the bus to school.

Off to School

To start the school day out right, most Puerto Rican kids eat a healthy breakfast of scrambled eggs, sausage, or French toast. They dress in school uniforms. Girls usually wear a jumper and a blouse. Boys put on short pants and a polo shirt in school colors. When boys get older, they trade in their shorts for long pants. Classes of 30 or 40 students are common. Kids may start learning English in kindergarten. Students also study history, art, music, computers, math, and science.

Schoolgirls on a field trip to Ponce

Baseball Bonanza!

Baseball is big in Puerto Rico! Kids love the game. Most big cities have baseball teams. Fans flock to stadiums to watch the games. Some Puerto Rican baseball players have joined major-league teams in the United States.

Basketball is another favorite sport among Puerto Rican athletes.

Batter up! Hopeful ballplayers (left) practice for the pros.

Roberto Clemente

Puerto Rican–born baseball player Roberto Clemente (1934–1972) was one of the best ballplayers ever! He helped the Pittsburgh Pirates win two World Series. In 1966 the U.S. National Baseball League named him Most Valuable Player. Clemente gave time and money to many Puerto Rican charities. After his death in 1972, the Puerto Rican government honored his memory by building the Roberto Clemente Sports City in his hometown, Carolina. There kids can take part in sports and other activities.

Salsa musicians groove to music that gets crowds on their feet.

Feel the Beat

The spicy dance music of Puerto Rico is called salsa. Musicians blend African and Caribbean rhythms with big-band jazz. Salsa bands feature several singers, a piano, a bass (large stringed instrument), trumpets, trombones, and saxophones. Musicians add a beat by shaking maracas (rattles) or tapping cowbells. Others beat drums such as bongos and congas.

The annual Pablo Casals Music Festival honors an important Puerto Rican classical musician.

Dear Mom and Dad,

Puerto Rico is rocking! Last night after dinner, Grandma and Grandpa took us to hear a salsa band. I could not sit still. Grandma has some salsa instruments at home. Both came from the Taino Indians. The *güiro* is a dried gourd with notches in it. When you drag a stick across it, it makes a cool scratching sound. The maracas are dried-out gourds with the seeds still in them. When you shake them, they rattle. Cha-cha-cha!

Love,

Rita

Bookworms

Puerto Ricans come from a rich tradition of storytelling. Many Taino and African tales explain how the world came to be. Spaniards told stories of witches and princesses. Early Puerto Rican authors wrote about the jíbaros. Others wrote about Puerto Rico's

Beautiful scenery inspires Puerto Rico's authors.

Puerto Ricans honor the jíbaro in stories and festivals.

beautiful landscape. Modern writers tell stories of Puerto Ricans living in New York City and how they adjust to new ways of life.

Juan Bobo

Juan Bobo (Simple John) is a well-known jíbaro story character. He gets into funny situations. In one story, he dresses the family pig in his mother's best clothes. In another he yells at a three-legged pot for being lazy. Juan thinks that a pot with three legs should be able to walk faster than he can.

39

Looks complicated! A weaver braids dozens of bobbins (wooden spools wrapped with thread) to create mundillo— *handmade lace.*

A woodworker carefully carves a piece of wood into the shape of a saint.

Arts and Crafts

Mask making is popular all over Puerto Rico. The most famous creations come from artists in the towns of Ponce and Loíza. People wearing masks with faces of scary devils, crazy-looking animals, and imaginary

Mask making is a traditional art form of the Taino, Spanish, and African peoples.

creatures dance down Puerto Rico's streets during the many parades and festivals.

Other artists make *santos* (saints) out of wood. Called *santeros*, these crafty carvers create detailed figures and religious scenes. Handmade lace is another popular craft. Weavers' fast-moving fingers form fancy lace out of thread.

Underground rivers helped shape the beautiful caves of Río Camuy Cave Park.

Vacation, Anyone?

After school and on weekends, Puerto Ricans fill nearby parks and beaches. City folks might spend long vacations visiting friends and family in the countryside. Beaches offer fun to swimmers, surfers, and snorkelers. Visitors to the Río Camuy Cave Park can explore the earth underground. Others might tour the rain forest or hike in the mountains.

A surfer catches a ride on a wave.

Paso Fino

Horse lovers have fun at the Paso Fino Festival held every March in the town of Guayama. During the festival, riders compete on horseback in a series of events. Spaniards brought *paso fino* horses, known for their gracefulness, to Puerto Rico. A group of these horses runs wild on Vieques.

New Words to Learn

ancestor: A relative who lived long ago.

bilingual: Someone able to speak two languages with ease.

cove: A small, shallow inlet.

crater: A hole in the ground shaped like a bowl.

ethnic group: A group of people with many things in common, such as language, religion, and customs.

ethnic Puerto Rican: A person who has ancestors from one or more of Puerto Rico's early ethnic groups—native Taino, African, and Spanish.

fortress: A building with strong walls that protects against an enemy.

hurricane: A big storm with strong winds and heavy rain.

island: A piece of land surrounded by water.

mountain range: A series, or group, of mountains—the parts of the earth's surface that rise high into the sky.

rain forest: A thick, green forest that gets lots of rain.

San Juan offers tourists a taste of old and new Puerto Rico.

tropical: Describes a region with a yearly weather condition that is usually hot and in which lots of rain falls.

U.S. commonwealth: A territory that was once ruled by the United States and that is still under its control to some degree.

New Words to Say

Arecibo	(ah-ray-SEE-boh)
asopao	(ah-soh-POW)
bayetes	(bah-YAY-tays)
Borinquén	(boh-reen-KAYN)
colmado	(cohl-MAH-doh)
Cordillera Central	(cohr-dee-YAY-rah sehn-TRAHL)
el coquí	(ehl koh-KEE)
El Yunque	(ehl YOON-kay)
español	(ays-pahn-YOHL)
güiro	(GWEE-roh)
inglés	(een-GLAYS)
jíbaro	(HEE-bah-roh)
La Fortaleza	(lah fohr-tah-LAY-zah)
Nuyoricans	(noo-yoh-REE-kahns)
Ponce	(POHN-say)
Puerto Rico	(PWAYR-toh REE-koh)
San Juan	(SAHN WAHN)
Sierra de Luquillo	(SYAY-rah day loo-KEE-yoh)
Taino	(TIE-noh)
tostones	(tohs-TOH-nays)
Vieques	(VYAY-kays)

More Books to Read

Belpré, Pura. *Firefly Summer.* Houston: Piñata Books, 1996.

Bernier-Grand, Carmen T. *Juan Bobo: Four Folktales from Puerto Rico.* New York: HarperTrophy, 1995.

London, Jonathan. *Hurricane!* New York: Lothrop, Lee & Shepard Books, 1998.

Mohr, Nicolasa. *The Song of El Coquí and Other Tales of Puerto Rico.* New York: Viking, 1995.

Nodar, Carmen Santiago. *Abuelita's Paradise.* Morton Grove, IL: A. Whitman, 1992.

Picó, Fernando. *The Red Comb.* Mahwah, NJ: Bridgewater Books, 1991.

Pitre, Felix (story retold by). *Juan Bobo and the Pig.* New York: Lodestar Books, 1993.

Puerto Rico. Minneapolis: Lerner Publications Company, 1994.

Ramirez, Michael Rose. *The Legend of the Hummingbird: A Tale from Puerto Rico.* Greenvale, NY: Mondo Publishing, 1998.

Souza, D. M. *Hurricanes.* Minneapolis: Carolrhoda Books, Inc., 1996.

New Words to Find